Gold, The Forgotten Resource

A Biblical and practical approach to gaining wealth through the acquisition of gold.

By Pastor Harry J Riley

1

TABLE OF CONTENT

Foreword

Introduction

2

3

FOREWORD

This is one of the most informative and

thought provoking books that I have ever

read on the

subject of gold and the biblical perspective

of it.

Pastor Riley has nailed this one and it is my

opinion that few people have taken the

opportunity

to explore the subject in this manner. I can truly say that reading this book has encouraged me in

a number of ways and it is my new objective to look at gold and the acquisition of it in a

different manner.

This book is a must- read even if you have never considered the purchase of gold and it

appears to be prophetic in its orientation.

Thank you Pastor Riley for having a concern for the welfare of people and for providing

us

with such an informed book to read. We are forever grateful for the ideas and information on the pages of this book.

Enjoy!

Elder Raymond Puryear- VIP, Karatbars International

Derek Brown-Gold Director Elite 3- Karatbars International

INTRODUCTION

Revelation 3:17-18 (AMPC)

17 For you say, I am rich; I have prospered *and* grown wealthy, and I am in need of nothing; and you do not realize *and* understand that you are wretched, pitiable, poor, blind, and naked.

18 Therefore I counsel you to purchase from Me gold refined *and* tested by fire, that you may be [truly] wealthy, and white clothes to clothe you and to keep the shame

of your nudity from being seen, and salve to put on your eyes, that you may see.

I have spent countless hours studying and preaching the word of God. I have taught on practically every subject from the bible known to man, but it was not until recently that I received a revelation from God on this passage. There it was, available to me for many years and yet it sat on the pages of my bible until God said it was time for me and you to have this revelation. While it is not a new revelation, it is a NOW revelation.

There are people who will debate me on the revelation that GOD gave me on this passage and to you, I say at least consider that this passage is more than symbolical of that which is pure and invincible within our hearts. Allow me to appeal to your sense of understanding and revelation. God never does or has produced anything that did not have purpose, and more specifically purpose that He could use for his glory. The problem is then that the foes, even Satan, would want us to be ignorant to yet another provision from God because of its potential to advance the kingdom of God. So, here we are and Revelations is saying to us, God challenges us to follow his instructions to "to buy from Me gold refined in the fire, that you may be rich"; and white garments, that you may be clothed, *that* the shame of your nakedness" may not be revealed; and anoint your eyes with eye salve, that you may see. This book purposely focuses on the Gold because it is my belief and revelation that God wants us to be rich, and that, the resource He wants to use is Gold. This may not hit you just yet, but keep reading and you will understand why Satan has kept this message from us over the centuries and now God is releasing it in the earth to us who believe. Read this book with an open mind and anticipation of revelation that will make you rich for the glory of God.

Deuteronomy8:18 (AMPC)

[18] But you shall [earnestly] remember the Lord your God, for it is He Who gives you power to get wealth, that He may establish His covenant which He swore to your fathers, as it is this day.

Pastor Harry Riley

CHAPTER I

The Beginning of Gold According to The World Systems

If you are a believer, you will get the revelation that there are two systems that exist; one is the system of the world, and the other is the system of God, or Kingdom of God. You don't hear much about the latter because we are dominated by the system of the world who does things according to its father Satan. After all, Satan was given the name "God of this world." (2 Corinthians 4:4) The world system does things without regard to integrity, fairness, justice, love, Gods law or even equality. It is a system that was designed to steal the hearts of men and appeal to their greed and inner unredeemed selfish ways. It has no boundaries and there are no godly rules. It is based on greed and deception and it is apparent even more in the 21st century as we see the rising number of scandals and injustices that run rampant.

So, just what is the story according to man and the world system? Like every other story that has been fed to us, it is filled with deception and lies designed to keep the world in bondage and reserve the "

"haves" and push the "have-not's" to the side.

According to an article published in ATS Bullion, (https://www.atsbullion.com/latest/2017/10/where-does-gold-come-from-and-how-is-gold-formed/, gold is produced by a supernova. A supernova is the final part of the star's existence from a mighty explosion. According to this article, the explosion propels lots of dust into the atmosphere which contains rich elements like magnesium, and iron, and it is from this process known as nucleosynthesis that gold is formed. It is further said that the process does not produce gold immediately, but that the dust which was spewed out from past generations begins to condense and washes in with the elements and sinks into the core along with heavy metals, and as the earth cools the gold is produced.

There is yet another theory that says that gold was formed when two neutron stars collided. Really? In fact, this theory suggests that these stars, which are eight times more massive than the Sun, collided and a powerful explosion occurred which created the gold and other heavy metals. Are we to believe such? There are so many questions that would have to be answered if we did. But, at any rate that is the story the world offers to us.

Since the discovery of gold, the world system has taken it and used it for jewelry, computers, cell phones, dentistry, medicine and even space exploration; but still it has found its way into the hands of scandal and shame. There are so many articles that exist that share how this precious metal provided to us by God, in many instances became the subject of scandal and crime. But, that's usually how things that the world embraces and decides to pollute end up.

Chapter II

The Beginning of Gold According to the Word of God

To understand the origin of a thing you don't ask the users of that thing. Instead, you ask the creator of that thing. Regardless to which standard you subscribe to (the standard of God or the standard of man), you will have to at least give careful consideration to what God says about Gold.

I will share several passages that will help

me explain it more from a biblical

perspective throughout this chapter.

To begin with, here are a few:

Genesis 2:11

The name of the first [is] Pison: that [is] it
which compasseth the whole land of
Havilah, where [there is] gold;

Genesis 2:12

And the gold of that land [is] good: there [is]
bdellium and the onyx stone.

Genesis 13:2

And Abram [was] very rich in cattle, in
silver, and in gold.

Genesis 24:22

"And it came to pass, as the camels had done drinking, that the man took a golden earring of half a shekel weight, and two bracelets for her hands of ten *shekels* weight of gold;"

It is at this point that I have to introduce the ideas that:

- Gold was God's idea and not a result of some big bang theory;
- Gold was not meant to be coveted or hoarded; and

- Gold was not exclusive to certain classe and races.

So, we begin by saying again that our biblical account of gold indicates that it was the first form of money and that God placed it in the garden and said it was good. If we read Genesis 2:12 we will see these wonderful words;

"And the gold of that land is good; bdellium and onyx stone are there." Note, He placed the gold there and then said that it is "of the land." In other words, it is produced from the land because I placed it in the land. By the virtue of God's capability of laying out the universe, He placed it in the land. No big bang theory! No atomic collision! No settling dust! Pure and simple, He placed it in the land. The challenge for mankind is that they don't know all of the places it was placed, just the ones that they discovered. By the way, if Eden is in Africa and if Africa has the largest source of gold in the world...... well I will let you figure that part out.

Gold was so important to God that He inspired the writers to mention it 417 times. In fact, it was often used for money which is mentioned 140 times and there was no currency as we know it.

May I add that the people of real wealth that are listed in the bible were always associated with gold and the amount of it that they had.

The value of gold in biblical times and still today, is the fact that it is rare. Furthermore, the fact that gold has a beautiful color, resists oxidation or tarnish and makes for beautiful jewelry makes it valuable as well. But one of the things that is seldom overlooked, is the fact that owning gold in both the Old and the New Testaments was compared to acquiring knowledge, wisdom and faith which makes it even more valuable to those of us who believe.

There were allowable uses of this precious metal in the times of old and even now. To begin with, God placed it in the earth and man was able to access it for his use and the glory of God. In Exodus 25:8,11, God himself commanded Moses to have the Israelites build a tabernacle for Him. The tabernacle contained 2204.85 pounds of gold amongst other metals. It is estimated that the temple of Solomon was made up of over 3000 tons of gold. In fact, the lampstand, utensil, forks, bowls, pitchers, basins, cups and other items were made of gold and silver (1 Chronicles 22:14). In the Most Holy, there were cherubs and an altar of incense that was made of gold. Even the house was overlaid with gold. If we were to use today's price of $1203 per oz., the gold in Solomon's temple would be worth $144 billion.

There is no question that tangible wealth has always been based upon the possession of how much gold or silver a person owns. There was no currency and gold and silver were the standards.

In biblical times, the gold was used for storage, wealth and value and the silver was used to trade daily. Having stated all of these facts, we would have to at least consider that gold has a divine significance as well as a monetary one. I say divine because it was mentioned during creation in Genesis 2.

"And a river went out of Eden to water the garden; and from thence it was parted, and became into four heads. The name of the first is Pison: that is, it which compasseth the whole land of Havilah, where there is gold; And the gold of that land is good."

God created the world and the elements that it contains and gold was one of them.

God created it so it has to be a product of

God. He did not design gold to be worshiped

or cherished, rather He designed it to

exemplify His glory and provision. Gold is

intrinsically valuable and beautiful. Gold

was God's provision to man and God had

the foresight to know in His infinite wisdom

that it would always hold its value. Gold, as

a matter of fact, was the standard of

monetary trade. Outside of gold and silver

there was no such thing as money back in

the times of old. Gold and silver were

synonymous with money. In Hebrew, there

was no word for money. When we read

passages in the scripture that refer to money,

they are referring to a unit of weight in gold,

silver or another metal.

We could easily conclude that God

placed gold and silver strategically on earth

around the world and that His intent was that

it be used by all mankind and accessible to

the rich and poor alike.

This is a wonderful thought; but

tragically the world system removed gold

and silver from its monetary role within the

last century. When that happened it created

an imbalance in our economy and our

currency now fluctuates in value. Artificial

wealth is created when the banks expand

their balance sheets. Monetary inflation and

interest rates that are low enrich the wealthy

but rob the poor of labor and savings. How

unbiblical this practice is as God hates

deceit and manipulation. The world system

promotes it but God hates it.

Gold was created by God to be the

backbone of economic growth and a

successful society because they balance a

perfect unit of measurement. Currency does not. God was so brilliant that He created the earth and placed fixed qualities of metals in it so that we could experience a perfect economy and not inflation or deflation. The world system messed it up when they abolished the Gold Standard in 1933 and made buying gold unlawful in the United States from 1933-1975. The grace of God has made it possible that we can now buy gold and create our own wealth, as God intended.

CHAPTER III

The Jewish Nation; God's Chosen and How They Were Robbed of Their Gold

One of the greatest, yet seldom discussed thefts in history took place between 1939-1945 and involved God's chosen nation, the

Jews, and gold. Few speak of this theft but I think it is important to understand that gold was seemingly one of the factors. If we are to believe that the Jews are God's chosen nation and that we are spiritually grafted in through the redemption of Christ, then we must believe that this event affected us as well. So what happened and why?

First, the thing that makes this theft so treacherous is the fact that it was conducted by a government; specifically, the government of Nazi Germany. This government stole around $580 million of gold from central bank which would be worth $5.6 billion in today's prices. Primarily this gold came from Jews who were murdered in concentration camps. These Jews had everything taken from them including the gold fillings in their teeth.

German troops invaded countries across Europe in the late 1930s and the early 1940s and while doing so they looted central bank and stole hundreds of tons of gold for the sake of financing their war. This to some is speculative, but it is widely believed that they exhausted their funds and had to steal the gold to finance their war. They then sold the gold to Switzerland, Portugal, and Sweden and to add injury to insult, it is believed that these countries knew the gold was stolen from the Jews.

When the war was over the allies recovered large quantities of gold that had been taken from people, who were in some cases killed in the death camps. At some point the collected gold was kept separate and used to help survivors, but then the United States, Britain and France decided that the gold bars should be treated as money and distributed it to the ten

governments that claimed that they had

major losses. Furthermore, they denied

individuals who claimed to have lost this

gold, any rights to the gold; citing that there

would be too many small claims for them to

settle. The three powers then set up a Gold

Commission to examine the claims from the

government of Albania, Austria, Belgium,

Czechoslovakia, Greece, Italy, Luxembourg,

The Netherlands, Poland and Yugoslavia.

The total amount of gold bars that was made

available to the commission was about 337

tons; which was not enough to serve everyone and could only substantiate about 64% of the validated claims.

There is still speculation that there is more gold that should have been recovered and a conference has been put together to determine if that is true. Skeptics doubt that we will ever know the true amount of gold that was stolen, and worse, many of the families who lost loved ones and gold may never recover what was once theirs.

What a sad commentary this is for the Jewish nation; and all over what appears to be the criminal act of stealing gold. Gold has financed many wars and provided the necessary means to cure debts; but unfortunately it has cost the lives of many undeserving citizens who unknowingly were to later become victims of those who misunderstood the purpose and plan that God had for gold. May we use the resource of God for wealth, but never take on the greed that often comes with the desire to use that resource for wealth.

CHAPTER IV

SOLOMON'S GOLD

Up to this point we have been talking about gold, but we have not provided you with a good view of a real person who amassed it. May I present to you Solomon.

Solomon is said to have been the richest man in the history of the world and according to many, not even the wealth of Bill Gates can compare to the wealth of Solomon. What is fascinating to me is that a large part of his wealth was in gold.

King Solomon ruled Israel after his father David. His reign was said to have been one of unprecedented prosperity that came from the wisdom that God gave to him. When Solomon received the wisdom of God, he reorganized his kingdom into 12 districts that cut across many boundaries and centralized the power in Jerusalem.

Solomon was without question the richest man in the world and there is little doubt that gold was a large part of that. We are not told the true value of his gold or silver but we do have an idea of how much gold he owned. I Kings 10:14-15 records that he received twenty-five tons of gold every year. When we consider that talents

were used as measurement of weight and
money (gold); we can say that a talent would
weigh roughly 75 U.S pounds (34.3
kilograms) which equals 1,094 troy ounces.
If we use $1,500 per troy ounce, a talent of
gold in today's value would be worth
$1,641,000 ,at $1,600 per troy ounce which
makes it worth $1,750,000.00. So if he
received 666 talents of metal each year, the
value of what he received each year would
be $1, 165, 766, 400.00 in U.S. dollars.

By now your mouth is hanging open,
but consider the fact that he was so rich that

gold and silver were as common as stones in
Jerusalem (2 Chronicles 1:15, 1King 10:27).

We know that he ruled over Israel for
forty years and that he brought in about 1.1
Billion dollars of gold each year. We can't
even calculate the amount of gold that he
received from kings and governors who did
business with him.

The point I am making here is that God
gave him wisdom and that wisdom led to the

acquisition of gold which was a large part of his wealth. With that in mind, it is definitely time for you and I to think about the blessing of gold in his life and understand that God has no respect of person. He did it for Solomon and He will do it for you and I. Solomon used his wisdom to acquire and manage his gold. We must do the same.

V

Gold, the Resource Prophetically Spoken
of for the Last Days

Believe it or not, gold has a place in the

fulfillment of prophesy for the last days. To

understand where gold fits in the scheme of

biblical prophecy, we must understand a few facts as follows:

- In 1961 the USA started having an issue having enough gold to back its dollar. Germany and Japan had the largest surpluses of Gold and dollars but the USA had the greatest deficit in governmental history and a greater debt than all the world combined.

- Foreign aid programs drain the U.S. Treasury and as we spend to supply services and to support troops in foreign countries, our dollars flowing

out of the U.S. Treasury, combined

with heavy taxes, public and private

debt and no gold to back our own

currency, has put us in a place of

potential bankruptcy. How does the

richest nation border bankruptcy?

- France cashed in dollars and caused

  a crisis in the USA. In 1971, the US

  went off the gold standard as a result

  and at the same time made a deal

  with Saudi Arabia to price oil in

  dollars. This stopped foreigners from

being able to redeem US dollars from the USA Treasury, and allowed oil to be bought with dollars

- On the 16th of April 2019, it was reported that German households are placing more interest in gold (Germany by the way virtually owns USA).

- Private individual owns 8,918 tons of gold which has increased by 246 tons since 2016.

- Three quarters of all Germans say they own gold in the form of jewelry, coins or investments.

- Every German over the age of 18 has an average of 58 grams of gold in the form of Jewelry and 71 grams in the form of bars or coins.

Why do you think this is? Do they know something that we don't? Let's go further as follows:

- August 15, 1971, President Nixon revealed his economic plan and stated that part of his strategy

included cutting loose the dollar

from gold which would then simply

allow it to do whatever in the foreign

transaction arena, until the natural

market decided its best value.

- There is a consideration for the

  European Common Currency to be

  the next successor to the dollar, and

  guess what Europe uses for its back

  up? Yep, Gold!

Here is the concern; the gold standard is about 100 years old and is a product of evolution. The concern is that we live in a world of sovereign powers and if there is no standard to finance international trade and domestic currency there is a problem. It is inevitable that the currency system as we know it will soon be done away with in exchange for a new system that fits more in line with the one world government system and the new world order. Both of which are part of end time prophecy.

So currency will be a thing of the past, but gold has the confidence of more people than any other standard. But don't take my word for it, let me show you an article about inflation that was written in 1981, by Curry, J and entitled, "How gold, inflation and government impact you." Outdated you may say. No, it is prophetic!

Why Gold?

"What does uncertainty in the world's financial system portend for the future? How will it affect you? And what about the value of gold? Gold has been the most sought after form of money for thousands of years. By universally accepted definition, money is anything that serves as a store of value and as a medium of exchange. Historically, gold has fit that description better than anything else. Because it is relatively scarce, virtually indestructible and possesses a wide range of artistic and functional uses, gold became the standard in most economies. It was easily coined, highly portable and universally recognized for its value.

Even though the supply of gold is limited, demand for the metal seems to be infinite.

Commodities such as food crops or industrial output can have price swings based on demand, weather, poor economic policies or disasters. None of these affect the total supply of gold. It maintains its value in relation to other commodities regardless. Thus it has acted as a financial constraint and stabilizing factor. People trust gold because it has been an instrument of monetary discipline and a standard of measure by which to measure other commodities.

Gold acts as a check on governments and politicians. Paper money came into use because it was more convenient to use than gold.

However, historically the amount of paper money in circulation was tied to the amount of gold a nation possessed. When people knew that gold backed up their currency, they trusted their money. But even though people may trust gold, they don't necessarily trust their leaders. In the words of George Bernard Shaw: "The most important thing about money is to maintain its stability....

With paper money this stability has to be maintained by the government. With a gold currency, it tends to maintain itself.... You have to choose as a voter between trusting the natural stability of gold and the natural stability of the honesty and intelligence of the members of the government. And, with due respect for these gentlemen, I advise you, as long as the capitalist system lasts, to vote for gold." The goal of every political leader is to remain in power. In a democracy, he must retain his popularity to be reelected.

Extravagant social welfare schemes and public works help to perpetuate the government's power, even though the country may not be able to afford the expense. If a political leader can get rid of the gold standard, then there is no restraint on the amount of paper money the government can print. The deficit between collected taxes and government spending can be made up through printing extra money. But the effect of these shortsighted policies soon becomes apparent. More and more paper money chases the available goods and services — the result is inflation.

Witness the situation in the United States

today. Since 1971 the dollar has had no

relationship to gold.

Multibillion dollar deficits in government

spending have been covered by printing

extra dollars. Because the dollar is not

convertible to gold, there is no check on

government spending and the citizens suffer

from consequent inflation. Inflation

becomes a vicious circle with everyone

eventually losing. As Voltaire concluded,

"All paper eventually returns to its intrinsic value — zero."

I could go on and on about the number of articles that speak of a devaluation of currency in this society and I would likely overwhelm you. But I must note, that as prophecy goes, the Bible does not show a significant value of gold until the first few couple of years of the Great Tribulation. Let me share a few prophecies that support that thought as follows:

40 "At the time of the end...43 He shall have

power over the treasures of gold and silver

(Daniel 11:40,43)

14... And the wealth of all the surrounding

nations shall be gathered together:

Gold, silver, and apparel in great abundance.

(Zechariah 14:14)

12 ... merchandise of gold and silver,

precious stones and pearls ... 16 ... 'Alas,

alas, that great city that was clothed in fine

linen, purple, and scarlet, and adorned with

gold and precious stones and pearls!
(Revelation 18:12, 16)

4 The woman was arrayed in purple and scarlet, and adorned with gold and precious stones and pearls (Revelation 17:4)

What is said here of gold is not said of currency anywhere. In Daniel 11:24, we can conclude that the leader mentioned will likely accumulate wealth prior to the Tribulation Period and it is likely that the accumulation involves gold.

I said earlier that Germany basically owns the USA. In February of 2017, Germany announced that it repatriated more of its gold more than three years ahead of time. We can suspect that this happened because nations are accumulating gold with the intention of devaluating the U.S. dollar as the world's reserve currency; and why not if a new world order is being planned.

It is unfortunate the U.S. is still unprepared for a plan that will devaluate and possibly dominate the present currency.

As if this thought wasn't concerning enough, add to it that the U.S. trade sanctions on China, Russia and Europe are starting to take their toll. Trump's new sanctions on Iran may very well be the straw that breaks the camel's back as the rest of the world tire of his (the U.S) bullying.

There are several things clear about this new world leader and one fact is that he is interested in gold in the end times. Gold will hold its value when the US dollar declines and eventually has no value.

This leader is aware of what we all need to understand about gold. Gold has been the most sought after form of money for thousands of years. Money is anything that serves as a store of value and exchange; gold fits that description. Gold is scarce, indestructible and has a wide range of functional uses. These attributes alone have allowed for gold to act as a financial constraint and stabilizer.

The truth is; paper money only came into use because it was more convenient to use than gold and yet historically the amount of paper money in circulation was always tied to the amount of gold a nation possessed.

Gold is the answer. I am not a fan of the one world government system as I know it is part of the beast system and that it is designed to control and manipulate people. On the other hand, it is a good system that possibly offers one national treasury, one currency and one monetary system.

The Bible does prophesy about a supreme world government but it will not come about through the efforts of man, but through man as it is part of the return of Christ.

We all see how little the dollar means now as compared to years ago. As such we are now questioning the fate of the dollar bill and as we do, we look to gold to be that next currency. At the worst case, it will not be eliminated and will maintain value to the holders.

I, like many of my friends, subscribe to the notion that when the U.S dollar totally collapses we can find refuge in the gold that we own. The collapse of the USA dollar will shake a lot of confidence in non-backed currency, but currency backed by gold will prove to be safer and more valuable. Now is the time to take heed because the day is coming where paper currency will have little to no value.

VI

Your Dollar Has No Real Value, But Gold Does

When I was a child, a dollar would purchase a lot from the grocery store. That is certainly not the case now and we have seen the decrease in the value of a dollar over the years. If I had to describe the dollar bill, I would say that it is nothing more than a piece of paper with little to no value. The Federal Reserve calls the dollar bill a note. In fact, it calls it a "Federal Reserve Note."

A note in banking terms is a debt and an IOU that says it will pay its lender back according to the terms of the note.

On the other hand, in the past we used a "Silver Certificate," that clearly spelled out the terms of the contract and stated that there was on deposit in the treasury of the United States of America, one dollar in silver, payable to the bearer on demand. Do you see the difference?

In 1935, the dollar was an honest measurement and tangible item for redeeming silver. Not today though. Today's dollar only has the statement that says, "This note is legal tender for all debts public or private."

The dollar has declined 95% in value since 1913. That means, what $100 bought back in 1913, today it would take $2,000.00 to buy.

We were taught to invest in CD's at the local bank and many heeded the advice and purchased some. The truth is though, that if we opened a CD that paid around 1.5%

annually we would actually be losing around 1.5% per year on our money. This would be due to a 3% inflation rate. But if we had taken that same money in 1913 and purchased gold, the value of that gold today would be $33,000.00.

One of the challenges of paper money is that it expands consumption way beyond income. When this happens debt collapse and social breakdown is in evitable. The foundation of the household collapses and the middle class is destroyed. Paper money is nothing more than an illusion because it is non-substance and is created by the government indefinitely. When we accept numbers on a green piece of paper, we are accepting an illusion of reality. Real money, gold and silver, comes from earth and human production not some illusive piece of paper created by man and given a false value.

The only way to a true economic growth experience is by transfer of services, goods, or wealth between people. Hence, gold. Buy gold! Here is how it works, people provide service and gets gold in return as compensation. In that case, both the service provider and the person who produced are benefited and they both have bettered their standard of living. It goes without saying that the one who produced had to get his product from somewhere and that person also benefited. This is transfer at its best and it works because everyone benefits.

On the other hand, the Fed produces nothing but paper money which takes away from the producer. So, when it comes to what it actually does; we can say it steals from the wealth of the producer and then taxes them so it can provide more fake

money and credit. In the end, financial

collapse is inevitable. Add to this that the

Fed is concerned with public perception and

how to keep the crowd under control so that

there is no negative impact on banks and

you have a system that is not designed for

your wealth accumulation.

A second and primary concern of the

Fed is its control of public perceptions.

The Fed must keep the crowd quiet. It

positively does not want a panic and

run on the banks. The very last thing

central banks want is transparency. The

vested interest (the paper money

crowd) will color the news more and

more.

VII

Why the Bible Supports Investing in Gold

Some may say that there is no scripture that tells you right out to buy gold; but there are hundreds of passages that seem to support that owning gold was acceptable to God and an indication of a resource used for wealth.

From the many passages in the bible we can clearly see that families benefited from the acquisition of God. To begin with, gold is one of the oldest forms of money that was used back in the biblical times.

I find it particularly interesting that in the biblical times, gold was found in its native purity in gravel deposits and riverbeds. It was easily separated and recovered because of how heavy it was. The book of Job, chapter 28 verses 1, 2, and 6 all speak of what appears to be mining. To me that signifies that God wanted us to have access to it. It was not hidden to the point of no access.

I honestly believe that God created gold to be used in the same manner as money is being used today. When there was no paper money, there was gold. God did not design His money system to be one of corruption, but one of blessings. It became a corrupt system when man took it upon himself to substitute the usage of gold and silver for paper money that could be controlled by man. There is no secret that our country is in debt and that our financial system is hanging on by a thread. We cannot solve it by printing more money; because printing it is one thing, having the resources to back it is something different.

Haggai 2:8 clearly declares that the silver and the gold belong to God. So God put it here and He put it here for us to use as money. It was the perfect (and still is) medium of exchange and it could not be manufactured by a person. Only God could produce it. It was so important that it was included in the building of the temple. Gold and silver have never been worthless in the history of our nation. But currencies have come and gone. Both the Greek Empire and the Roman Empire had to reform themselves because their money system failed. But not gold.

I could make a case for owning gold and support it with many passages of the bible. I will stop short at saying that from Genesis to Revelations, we see where gold was significant. In the book of Genesis, which is the book of the creation process of GOD, we see that gold had a place there. Gold is said to have been available to Adam and Eve in abundance.

In 1 Corinthians, the Apostle suggests that it withstands fire and is used to emphasize wisdom, faith and knowledge of the word of God.

In the book of Revelations, which refers to recreation we see that gold was used to build the city. The point here is that nowhere in the bible does it condemn the ownership of gold, but it does show its many uses.

There are many people who will argue with me over my thoughts concerning gold. I only encourage them to explore for themselves and see what revelation GOD will give to them. Even if you decided that you are not interested in this revelation, it would not bother me at all, as I subscribe to the notion that every person is entitled to their own decision. I would hope that you would listen to me, but if not, I accept your decision.

I do have one last thought concerning the matter. There will come a time (and we can see it now), that gold will return to its true value as a resource that comes from God. God gave it to us and with it came an aesthetic value that cannot be replaced. It

has antibiotic properties that can be used in

many industries. Gold is a kingdom

provision and it was meant as a means of

wealth to the holder. All who were willing

to pay the price of labor for it could receive

it and experience the wealth of GOD here on

earth.

It is my belief that we too can experience

GOD's provision through this resource

know to us as gold. Kings owned it,

tabernacles were built with it, household and

even sacred objects were made of it. It

makes good sense to me that God has no

issue with us having and using it. What does

not make sense is why we were not told

about this in our educational institutes and

even from the pulpit. For what it's worth, I

am praying that you get the revelation and

the gold.

VIII

A Survey of the One World Government System and the Devaluation of Currency in this Century

Gold will prove to be of greater importance as we witness the one world government system and the mark of the beast. What is the one world government system and how does it play into the end time? While we were going on with life, the powers to be were putting it in place in preparation for the Anti-Christ and the end times.

As a part of the one world government system, the world bank which is now functioning to our unawares, has to devaluate the currency. What that means is that, in order to devaluate the currency; they have to lower the exchange rate by implementing a fixed exchange rate instead of one that changes. When that happens the dollar value decreases and ultimately ends. In concert with this anticipated move, the world has implemented what is known as the construction of the one world government system or better referred to as "new universal agenda." Most people have never heard of it and that is because it was not meant for the public to know about just yet.

The global elite came together some years ago and created the European Common Market Nations; who is at the center of these workings. There were a series of treaties made that interlocked international agreements designed to create one world governed by these entities that include a bank governed by the same.

The danger of this is not only that it is a part of the end time prophetic calendar but that it was designed to control us and our economy by this group of people who represent various nations who have aligned themselves to become one. There is not a lot of talk about this, which should raise suspicion in and of itself. What they did not tell us was that a few years ago the Pope traveled to New York to give the address for this new world order, and at the same time endorsed the construction of this one world system. Every nation on the planet signed up for the 17 goals of this new group. So, why wasn't it covered by our media? Because they did not want the world to know that they were putting together the system that will ultimately become a part of the last system before the world ends. Without God's input this group is seeking to unify us and turn this world around.

This system was spoken of in Daniel and other books and is an indication of preparation for the return of Christ. Gold may very well have its place when currency has no value during this time.

This group is insisting that the 17

sustainable development goals and the 169

sustainable targets designed to transform our

world be embraced by us all by 2030.

Through controlled media, we will be told

that this is all about saving our environment

and putting an end to poverty. In actuality,

this "Agenda 21," is designed to establish a

global government, global economic system

and global religion.

Some of the biggest names in the

music world promoted these new goals at

the Global Citizen Festival, that was held in

Central Park, and we did not even know
what was behind it. Stars and celebrities
including those in the religious world
continue to promote this agenda without us
even understanding what they are saying
because they use language that is familiar to
us laced with that agenda. They are now
training us to think of ourselves as global
citizens. Very powerful secret societies and
people are accepting these changes and we
are following along with them without even
knowing it. There are secret groups that pull
all the strings and we are missing what is

really taking place. All of this so that the world can become a 'single market' with uniform laws, rules and regulations. To many unawares, we are merging with other economies along with the rest of the world and in the process we are losing thousands of business and dollars as we watch this system dominate our economy. Take a look at the companies that are surfacing in the US and you will see that many of them are from Germany.

I could go on and on with this but suffice me to say that our economy is being high-jacked by a world system that looks the

part but in reality is designed toward our

demise. Gold, is our real friend and as the

dollar ceases to exist, gold will hold its

worth.

IX

Where Do I Start

If you read this book and you came to the conclusion that you really need to consider purchasing gold, you have managed to take the first step. The first step in any new process is always to change your mindset.

Now that you have changed your mindset and you are considering the need for you to secure your family and gain wealth through the acquisition of gold, I want to give you a little practical advice. There are thousands of companies and people who can help you with this process. At the risk of sounding like a broker, I can help you as well and even though that is not the purpose of this book, suffice it for me to say you can email me if you would like my advice.

Let's take a look at some practical advice.

1. Only buy physical gold or silver.

2. Make sure it is under your direct ownership. In other words, you must be able to hold it in your possession.

3. Buy as much as you can afford to build up your stock in case you need to liquidate.

4. Build up liquid stocks as a means of monetary insurance as well as a source of savings over a long period of time.

5. Don't use credit, buy with your savings.

6. Always keep your gold near you.

7. Never store your gold in a banking system.

8. Make sure you understand the laws when you buy.

9. Pay yourself first.

10. Save in gold with karatbars.

Those are just a few things that I think you should know. It goes without saying that to get a real understanding you should seek the help and advice of a person such as myself. You cannot go wrong investing in gold. It has and always will stand the test of time.

X

The Prayer for Wisdom in the Acquisition of God

Father in the name of Jesus, your kingdom is so valuable to me and I want to be a part of bringing your kingdom here on earth. At a time in his life when he wanted to make an impact in his land, Jabez asked you to bless him indeed and you answered his prayer. I come now Lord asking first for your wisdom. I need your wisdom as Solomon so that I may manage the resources that you give to me. I ask Lord that you bless me to acquire gold in a way I never imagined. I thank you that you are putting me in the right place to acquire gold. I thank you that you are giving me the resource for which to purchase it with and I thank you that you are helping me to purchase it at the right time, under the right circumstances.

Lord, I stand on your word and all the passages that support you blessing me in this manner. Lord I believe all 361 verses of your Bible that support your support of gold and I believe in my heart that it is the vehicle that you want to use to take me to a place of wealth.

Thank you Lord that you have created me in your image and that you have ordained for me to be a part of what you are doing in this end time.

Thank you that gold is yours and that as a loving father you willfully share it with your children so that they can conduct kingdom work and live the abundant life that you spoke of.

Thank you Lord that my desire is not for greed or any other means except to glorify your name.

Lord, I honor you and your word and I receive all the gold that I can store up this day in the name of Jesus. Amen

XI

Gold from Genesis to Revelations

Genesis 2:11

The name of the first [is] Pison: that [is] it which compasseth the whole land of Havilah, where [there is] gold;

Genesis 2:12

And the gold of that land [is] good: there [is] bdellium and the onyx stone.

Genesis 13:2

And Abram [was] very rich in cattle, in silver, and in gold.

And the LORD hath blessed my master greatly; and he is become great: and he hath given him flocks, and herds, and silver, and gold, and menservants, and maidservants, and camels, and asses.

Exodus 25:3

And this [is] the offering which ye shall take of them; gold, and silver, and brass,

Numbers 7:84

This [was] the dedication of the altar, in the day when it was anointed, by the princes of Israel: twelve chargers of silver, twelve silver bowls, twelve spoons of gold:

Numbers 7:86

The golden spoons [were] twelve, full of incense, [weighing] ten [shekels] apiece, after the shekel of the sanctuary: all the gold of the spoons [was] a hundred and twenty [shekels].

Numbers 24:13

If Balak would give me his house full of silver and gold, I cannot go beyond the commandment of the LORD, to do [either] good or bad of mine own mind; [but] what the LORD saith, that will I speak?

Numbers 31:22

Only the gold, and the silver, the brass, the iron, the tin, and the lead,

Numbers 31:50

We have therefore brought an oblation for the LORD, what every man hath gotten, of jewels of gold, chains, and bracelets, rings, earrings, and tablets, to make an atonement for our souls before the LORD.

Numbers 31:51

And Moses and Eleazar the priest took the gold of them, [even] all wrought jewels.

Numbers 31:52

And all the gold of the offering that they offered up to the LORD, of the captains of thousands, and of the captains of hundreds, was sixteen thousand seven hundred and fifty shekels.

Numbers 31:54

And Moses and Eleazar the priest took the gold of the captains of thousands and of hundreds, and brought it into the tabernacle of the congregation, [for] a memorial for the children of Israel before the LORD.

Deuteronomy 8:13

And [when] thy herds and thy flocks multiply, and thy silver and thy gold is multiplied, and all that thou hast is multiplied;

Deuteronomy 17:17

Neither shall he multiply wives to himself, that his heart turn not away: neither shall he greatly multiply to himself silver and gold.

Joshua 6:19

But all the silver, and gold, and vessels of brass and iron, [are] consecrated unto the LORD: they shall come into the treasury of the LORD.

Joshua 6:24

And they burnt the city with fire, and all that [was] therein: only the silver, and the gold, and the vessels of brass and of iron, they put into the treasury of the house of the LORD.

Samuel-1 6:8

And take the ark of the LORD and lay it
upon the cart; and put the jewels of gold,
which ye return him [for] a trespass offering,
in a coffer by the side thereof; and send it
away, that it may go.

Samuel-1 6:11

And they laid the ark of the LORD upon the
cart, and the coffer with the mice of gold
and the images of their emerods.

Samuel-2 8:10

Then Toi sent Joram his son unto king
David, to salute him, and to bless him,
because he had fought against Hadadezer,
and smitten him: for Hadadezer had wars
with Toi. And [Joram] brought with him
vessels of silver, and vessels of gold, and
vessels of brass:

Samuel-2 8:11

Which also king David did dedicate unto the
LORD, with the silver and gold that he had
dedicated of all nations which he subdued;

Samuel-2 12:30

And he took their king's crown from off his head, the weight whereof [was] a talent of gold with the precious stones: and it was [set] on David's head. And he brought forth the spoil of the city in great abundance.

Kings-1 6:21

So, Solomon overlaid the house within with pure gold: and he made a partition by the chains of gold before the oracle; and he overlaid it with gold.

Kings-1 6:22

And the whole house he overlaid with gold, until he had finished all the house: also, the whole altar that [was] by the oracle he overlaid with gold.

Kings-2 7:8

And when these lepers came to the uttermost part of the camp, they went into one tent, and did eat and drink, and carried thence silver, and gold, and raiment, and went and hid [it]; and came again, and entered into another tent, and carried thence [also], and went and hid [it].

Kings-2 12:13

Howbeit there were not made for the house of the LORD bowls of silver, snuffers, basins, trumpets, any vessels of gold, or vessels of silver, of the money [that was] brought into the house of the LORD:

Kings-2 12:18

And Jehoash king of Judah took all the hallowed things that Jehoshaphat, and Jehoram, and Ahaziah, his fathers, kings of Judah, had dedicated, and his own hallowed things, and all the gold [that was] found in the treasures of the house of the LORD, and in the king's house, and sent [it] to Hazael king of Syria: and he went away from Jerusalem.

Kings-2 14:14

And he took all the gold and silver, and all the vessels that were found in the house of the LORD, and in the treasures of the king's house, and hostages, and returned to Samaria.

Kings-2 16:8

And Ahaz took the silver and gold that was found in the house of the LORD, and in the treasures of the king's house, and sent [it for] a present to the king of Assyria.

Kings-2 18:14

And Hezekiah king of Judah sent to the king of Assyria to Lachish, saying, I have offended; return from me: that which thou puttest on me will I bear. And the king of Assyria appointed unto Hezekiah king of Judah three hundred talents of silver and thirty talents of gold.

Chronicles-1 18:11

Them also king David dedicated unto the LORD, with the silver and the gold that he brought from all [these] nations; from Edom, and from Moab, and from the children of Ammon, and from the Philistines, and from Amalek.

Chronicles-2 1:15

And the king made silver and gold at
Jerusalem [as plenteous] as stones, and
cedar trees made he as the sycamore trees
that [are] in the vale for abundance.

Chronicles-2 2:7

Send me now therefore a man cunning to
work in gold, and in silver, and in brass, and
in iron, and in purple, and crimson, and blue,
and that can skill to grave with the cunning
men that [are] with me in Judah and in
Jerusalem, whom David my father did
provide.

Chronicles-2 2:14

The son of a woman of the daughters of
Dan, and his father [was] a man of Tyre,
skilful to work in gold, and in silver, in
brass, in iron, in stone, and in timber, in
purple, in blue, and in fine linen, and in
crimson; also to grave any manner of
graving, and to find out every device which
shall be put to him, with thy cunning men,
and with the cunning men of my lord David
thy father.

Chronicles-2 3:4

And the porch that [was] in the front [of the house], the length [of it was] according to the breadth of the house, twenty cubits, and the height [was] an hundred and twenty: and he overlaid it within with pure gold.

Chronicles-2 3:5

And the greater house he ceiled with fir tree, which he overlaid with fine gold, and set thereon palm trees and chains.

Ezra 1:4

And whosoever remaineth in any place where he sojourneth, let the men of his place help him with silver, and with gold, and with goods, and with beasts, beside the freewill offering for the house of God that [is] in Jerusalem.

Ezra 1:6

And all they that [were] about them strengthened their hands with vessels of silver, with gold, with goods, and with beasts, and with precious things, beside all [that] was willingly offered.

Ezra 1:9

And this [is] the number of them: thirty chargers of gold, a thousand chargers of silver, nine and twenty knives,

Ezra 1:10

Thirty basins of gold, silver basins of a second [sort] four hundred and ten, [and] other vessels a thousand.

Ezra 1:11

All the vessels of gold and of silver [were] five thousand and four hundred. All [these] did Sheshbazzar bring up with [them of] the captivity that were brought up from Babylon unto Jerusalem.

Ezra 2:69

They gave after their ability unto the treasure of the work threescore and one thousand drams of gold, and five thousand pound of silver, and one hundred priests' garments.

Ezra 5:14

And the vessels also of gold and silver of the house of God, which Nebuchadnezzar took out of the temple that [was] in Jerusalem, and brought them into the temple of Babylon, those did Cyrus the king take out of the temple of Babylon, and they were delivered unto [one], whose name [was] Sheshbazzar, whom he had made governor;

Ezra 7:15*

And to carry the silver and gold, which the king and his counsellors have freely offered unto the God of Israel, whose habitation [is] in Jerusalem,

Ezra 7:16

And all the silver and gold that thou canst find in all the province of Babylon, with the freewill offering of the people, and of the priests, offering willingly for the house of their God which [is] in Jerusalem:

Ezra 7:18

And whatsoever shall seem good to thee, and to thy brethren, to do with the rest of the silver and the gold, that do after the will of your God.

And weighed unto them the silver, and the gold, and the vessels, [even] the offering of the house of our God, which the king, and his counsellors, and his lords, and all Israel [there] present, had offered:

Ezra 8:26

I even weighed unto their hand six hundred and fifty talents of silver, and silver vessels an hundred talents, [and] of gold an hundred talents;

Ezra 8:27

Also twenty basins of gold, of a thousand drams; and two vessels of fine copper, precious as gold.

Ezra 8:28

And I said unto them, Ye [are] holy unto the LORD; the vessels [are] holy also; and the silver and the gold [are] a freewill offering unto the LORD God of your fathers.

Ezra 8:30

So took the priests and the Levites the weight of the silver, and the gold, and the vessels, to bring [them] to Jerusalem unto the house of our God.

Ezra 8:33

Now on the fourth day was the silver and the gold and the vessels weighed in the house of our God by the hand of Meremoth the son of Uriah the priest; and with him [was] Eleazar the son of Phinehas; and with them [was] Jozabad the son of Jeshua, and Noadiah the son of Binnui, Levites;

Nehemiah 7:70

And some of the chief of the fathers gave unto the work. The Tirshatha gave to the treasure a thousand drams of gold, fifty basins, five hundred and thirty priests' garments.

Nehemiah 7:71

And [some] of the chief of the fathers gave to the treasure of the work twenty thousand drams of gold, and two thousand and two hundred pound of silver.

Nehemiah 7:72

And [that] which the rest of the people gave [was] twenty thousand drams of gold, and two thousand pound of silver, and threescore and seven priests' garments.

Esther 1:6

[Where were] white, green, and blue, [hangings], fastened with cords of fine linen and purple to silver rings and pillars of marble: the beds [were of] gold and silver, upon a pavement of red, and blue, and white, and black, marble.

Esther 1:7

And they gave [them] drink in vessels of gold, (the vessels being diverse one from another,) and royal wine in abundance, according to the state of the king.

Esther 8:15

And Mordecai went out from the presence of the king in royal apparel of blue and white, and with a great crown of gold, and with a garment of fine linen and purple: and the city of Shushan rejoiced and was glad.

Job 3:15

Or with princes that had gold, who filled their houses with silver:

Job 22:24

Then shalt thou lay up gold as dust, and the [gold] of Ophir as the stones of the brooks.

Job 23:10

But he knoweth the way that I take: [when] he hath tried me, I shall come forth as gold.

Job 28:1

Surely there is a vein for the silver, and a place for gold [where] they fine [it].

Job 28:6

The stones of it [are] the place of sapphires: and it hath dust of gold.

Job 28:15

It cannot be gotten for gold, neither shall silver be weighed [for] the price thereof.

Job 28:16

It cannot be valued with the gold of Ophir, with the precious onyx, or the sapphire.

<u>Job 28:17</u>

The gold and the crystal cannot equal it: and the exchange of it [shall not be for] jewels of fine gold.

<u>Job 28:19</u>

The topaz of Ethiopia shall not equal it, neither shall it be valued with pure gold.

<u>Job 31:24</u>

If I have made gold my hope, or have said to the fine gold, [Thou art] my confidence;

<u>Job 36:19</u>

Will he esteem thy riches? [no], not gold, nor all the forces of strength.

<u>Job 42:11</u>

Then came there unto him all his brethren, and all his sisters, and all they that had been of his acquaintance before, and did eat bread with him in his house: and they bemoaned him, and comforted him over all the evil that the LORD had brought upon him: every man also gave him a piece of money, and every one an earring of gold.

Psalms 19:10

More to be desired [are they] than gold, yea, than much fine gold: sweeter also than honey and the honeycomb.

Psalms 21:3

For thou preventest him with the blessings of goodness: thou settest a crown of pure gold on his head.

Psalms 45:9

Kings' daughters [were] among thy honourable women: upon thy right hand did stand the queen in gold of Ophir.

Psalms 45:13

The king's daughter [is] all glorious within: her clothing [is] of wrought gold.

Psalms 68:13

Though ye have lien among the pots, [yet shall ye be as] the wings of a dove covered with silver, and her feathers with yellow gold.

Psalms 72:15

And he shall live, and to him shall be given of the gold of Sheba: prayer also shall be made for him continually; [and] daily shall he be praised.

Psalms 105:37

He brought them forth also with silver and gold: and [there was] not one feeble [person] among their tribes.

Psalms 115:4

Their idols [are] silver and gold, the work of men's hands.

Psalms 119:72

The law of thy mouth [is] better unto me than thousands of gold and silver.

Psalms 119:127

Therefore I love thy commandments above gold; yea, above fine gold.

Psalms 135:15

The idols of the heathen [are] silver and gold, the work of men's hands.

Proverbs 3:14

For the merchandise of it [is] better than the merchandise of silver, and the gain thereof than fine gold.

Proverbs 8:10

Receive my instruction, and not silver; and knowledge rather than choice gold.

Proverbs 8:19

My fruit [is] better than gold, yea, than fine gold; and my revenue than choice silver.

Proverbs 11:22

[As] a jewel of gold in a swine's snout, [so is] a fair woman which is without discretion.

Proverbs 16:16

How much better [is it] to get wisdom than gold! and to get understanding rather to be chosen than silver!

Proverbs 17:3

The fining pot [is] for silver, and the furnace for gold: but the LORD trieth the hearts.

Proverbs 20:15

There is gold, and a multitude of rubies: but the lips of knowledge [are] a precious jewel.

Proverbs 22:1

A [good] name [is] rather to be chosen than great riches, [and] loving favour rather than silver and gold.

Proverbs 25:11

A word fitly spoken [is like] apples of gold in pictures of silver.

Proverbs 25:12

[As] an earring of gold, and an ornament of fine gold, [so is] a wise reprover upon an obedient ear.

Proverbs 27:21

[As] the fining pot for silver, and the furnace for gold; so [is] a man to his praise.

Ecclesiastes 2:8

I gathered me also silver and gold, and the peculiar treasure of kings and of the provinces: I gat me men singers and women singers, and the delights of the sons of men, [as] musical instruments, and that of all sorts.

Song-of-Solomon 1:10

Thy cheeks are comely with rows [of jewels], thy neck with chains [of gold].

Song-of-Solomon 1:11

We will make thee borders of gold with studs of silver.

Song-of-Solomon 3:10

He made the pillars thereof [of] silver, the bottom thereof [of] gold, the covering of it [of] purple, the midst thereof being paved [with] love, for the daughters of Jerusalem.

Song-of-Solomon 5:11

His head [is as] the most fine gold, his locks [are] bushy, [and] black as a raven.

Song-of-Solomon 5:14

His hands [are as] gold rings set with the beryl: his belly [is as] bright ivory overlaid [with] sapphires.

Song-of-Solomon 5:15

His legs [are as] pillars of marble, set upon sockets of fine gold: his countenance [is] as Lebanon, excellent as the cedars.

Isaiah 2:7

Their land also is full of silver and gold, neither [is there any] end of their treasures; their land is also full of horses, neither [is there any] end of their chariots:

Isaiah 2:20

In the day a man shall cast his idols of silver, and his idols of gold, which they made each one for himself to worship, to the moles and to the bats;

Isaiah 13:12

I will make a man more precious than fine gold; even a man than the golden wedge of Ophir.

Isaiah 13:17

Behold, I will stir up the Medes against them, which shall not regard silver; and [as for] gold, they shall not delight in it.

Isaiah 30:22

Ye shall defile also the covering of thy graven images of silver, and the ornament of thy molten images of gold: thou shalt cast them away as a menstruous cloth; thou shalt say unto it, Get thee hence.

Isaiah 31:7

For in that day every man shall cast away his idols of silver, and his idols of gold, which your own hands have made unto you [for] a sin.

Isaiah 39:2

And Hezekiah was glad of them, and showed them the house of his precious things, the silver, and the gold, and the spices, and the precious ointment, and all the house of his armour, and all that was found in his treasures: there was nothing in his house, nor in all his dominion, that Hezekiah showed them not.

Isaiah 40:19

The workman melteth a graven image, and the goldsmith spreadeth it over with gold, and casteth silver chains.

Isaiah 46:6

They lavish gold out of the bag, and weigh silver in the balance, [and] hire a goldsmith; and he maketh it a god: they fall down, yea, they worship.

Isaiah 60:6

The multitude of camels shall cover thee, the dromedaries of Midian and Ephah; all they from Sheba shall come: they shall bring gold and incense; and they shall show forth the praises of the LORD.

Isaiah 60:9

Surely the isles shall wait for me, and the ships of Tarshish first, to bring thy sons from far, their silver and their gold with them, unto the name of the LORD thy God, and to the Holy One of Israel, because he hath glorified thee.

Isaiah 60:17

For brass I will bring gold, and for iron I will bring silver, and for wood brass, and for stones iron: I will also make thy officers peace, and thine exactors righteousness.

Jeremiah 4:30

And [when] thou [art] spoiled, what wilt thou do? Though thou clothest thyself with crimson, though thou deckest thee with ornaments of gold, though thou rentest thy face with painting, in vain shalt thou make thyself fair; [thy] lovers will despise thee, they will seek thy life.

Jeremiah 10:4

They deck it with silver and with gold; they fasten it with nails and with hammers, that it move not.

Jeremiah 10:9

Silver spread into plates is brought from Tarshish, and gold from Uphaz, the work of the workman, and of the hands of the founder: blue and purple [is] their clothing: they [are] all the work of cunning [men].

Jeremiah 52:19

And the basins, and the firepans, and the bowls, and the caldrons, and the candlesticks, and the spoons, and the cups; [that] which [was] of gold [in] gold, and

[that] which [was] of silver [in] silver, took the captain of the guard away.

Lamentations 4:1

How is the gold become dim! [how] is the most fine gold changed! the stones of the sanctuary are poured out in the top of every street.

Lamentations 4:2

The precious sons of Zion, comparable to fine gold, how are they esteemed as earthen pitchers, the work of the hands of the potter!

Ezekiel 7:19

They shall cast their silver in the streets, and their gold shall be removed: their silver and their gold shall not be able to deliver them in the day of the wrath of the LORD: they shall not satisfy their souls, neither fill their bowels: because it is the stumblingblock of their iniquity.

Ezekiel 16:13

Thus wast thou decked with gold and silver; and thy raiment [was of] fine linen, and silk, and broidered work; thou didst eat fine flour, and honey, and oil: and thou wast exceeding beautiful, and thou didst prosper into a kingdom.

Ezekiel 16:17

Thou hast also taken thy fair jewels of my gold and of my silver, which I had given thee, and madest to thyself images of men, and didst commit whoredom with them,

Ezekiel 27:22

The merchants of Sheba and Raamah, they [were] thy merchants: they occupied in thy fairs with chief of all spices, and with all precious stones, and gold.

Ezekiel 28:4

With thy wisdom and with thine understanding thou hast gotten thee riches, and hast gotten gold and silver into thy treasures:

Ezekiel 28:13

Thou hast been in Eden the garden of God; every precious stone [was] thy covering, the sardius, topaz, and the diamond, the beryl, the onyx, and the jasper, the sapphire, the emerald, and the carbuncle, and gold: the workmanship of thy tabrets and of thy pipes was prepared in thee in the day that thou wast created.

Ezekiel 38:13

Sheba, and Dedan, and the merchants of Tarshish, with all the young lions thereof, shall say unto thee, Art thou come to take a spoil? hast thou gathered thy company to take a prey? to carry away silver and gold, to take away cattle and goods, to take a great spoil?

Daniel 2:32

This image's head [was] of fine gold, his breast and his arms of silver, his belly and his thighs of brass,

Daniel 2:35

Then was the iron, the clay, the brass, the silver, and the gold, broken to pieces together, and became like the chaff of the summer threshingfloors; and the wind carried them away, that no place was found for them: and the stone that smote the image became a great mountain, and filled the whole earth.

Daniel 2:38

And wheresoever the children of men dwell, the beasts of the field and the fowls of the heaven hath he given into thine hand, and hath made thee ruler over them all. Thou [art] this head of gold.

Daniel 2:45

Forasmuch as thou sawest that the stone was cut out of the mountain without hands, and that it brake in pieces the iron, the brass, the clay, the silver, and the gold; the great God hath made known to the king what shall come to pass hereafter: and the dream [is] certain, and the interpretation thereof sure.

Daniel 3:1

Nebuchadnezzar the king made an image of gold, whose height [was] threescore cubits, [and] the breadth thereof six cubits: he set it up in the plain of Dura, in the province of Babylon.

Daniel 5:4

They drank wine, and praised the gods of gold, and of silver, of brass, of iron, of wood, and of stone.

Daniel 5:7

The king cried aloud to bring in the astrologers, the Chaldeans, and the soothsayers. [And] the king spake, and said to the wise [men] of Babylon, Whosoever shall read this writing, and show me the interpretation thereof, shall be clothed with scarlet, and [have] a chain of gold about his neck, and shall be the third ruler in the kingdom.

Daniel 5:16

And I have heard of thee, that thou canst make interpretations, and dissolve doubts: now if thou canst read the writing, and make known to me the interpretation thereof, thou shalt be clothed with scarlet, and [have] a chain of gold about thy neck, and shalt be the third ruler in the kingdom.

Daniel 5:23

But hast lifted up thyself against the Lord of heaven; and they have brought the vessels of his house before thee, and thou, and thy lords, thy wives, and thy concubines, have drunk wine in them; and thou hast praised the gods of silver, and gold, of brass, iron, wood, and stone, which see not, nor hear, nor know: and the God in whose hand thy breath [is], and whose [are] all thy ways, hast thou not glorified:

Daniel 5:29

Then commanded Belshazzar, and they clothed Daniel with scarlet, and [put] a chain of gold about his neck, and made a proclamation concerning him, that he should be the third ruler in the kingdom.

Daniel 10:5

Then I lifted up mine eyes, and looked, and behold a certain man clothed in linen, whose loins [were] girded with fine gold of Uphaz:

Daniel 11:8

And shall also carry captives into Egypt their gods, with their princes, [and] with their precious vessels of silver and of gold; and he shall continue [more] years than the king of the north.

Daniel 11:38

But in his estate shall he honour the God of forces: and a god whom his fathers knew not shall he honour with gold, and silver, and with precious stones, and pleasant things.

Daniel 11:43

But he shall have power over the treasures of gold and of silver, and over all the precious things of Egypt: and the Libyans and the Ethiopians [shall be] at his steps.

Hosea 2:8

For she did not know that I gave her corn, and wine, and oil, and multiplied her silver and gold, [which] they prepared for Baal.

Hosea 8:4

They have set up kings, but not by me: they have made princes, and I knew [it] not: of their silver and their gold have they made them idols, that they may be cut off.

Joel 3:5

Because ye have taken my silver and my gold, and have carried into your temples my goodly pleasant things:

Nahum 2:9

Take ye the spoil of silver, take the spoil of gold: for [there is] none end of the store [and] glory out of all the pleasant furniture.

Habakkuk 2:19

Woe unto him that saith to the wood, Awake; to the dumb stone, Arise, it shall teach! Behold, it [is] laid over with gold and silver, and [there is] no breath at all in the midst of it.

Zephania 1:18

Neither their silver nor their gold shall be able to deliver them in the day of the LORD'S wrath; but the whole land shall be devoured by the fire of his jealousy: for he shall make even a speedy riddance of all them that dwell in the land.

Haggai 2:8

The silver [is] mine, and the gold [is] mine, saith the LORD of hosts.

Zecharia 4:2

And said unto me, What seest thou? And I said, I have looked, and behold a candlestick all [of] gold, with a bowl upon the top of it, and his seven lamps thereon, and seven pipes to the seven lamps, which [are] upon the top thereof:

Zecharia 6:11

Then take silver and gold, and make crowns, and set [them] upon the head of Joshua the son of Josedech, the high priest;

Zecharia 9:3

And Tyrus did build herself a strong hold, and heaped up silver as the dust, and fine gold as the mire of the streets.

Zecharia 13:9

And I will bring the third part through the fire, and will refine them as silver is refined, and will try them as gold is tried: they shall call on my name, and I will hear them: I will

say, It [is] my people: and they shall say,
The LORD [is] my God.

Zecharia 14:14

And Judah also shall fight at Jerusalem; and
the wealth of all the heathen round about
shall be gathered together, gold, and silver,
and apparel, in great abundance.

Malachi 3:3

And he shall sit [as] a refiner and purifier of
silver: and he shall purify the sons of Levi,
and purge them as gold and silver, that they
may offer unto the LORD an offering in
righteousness.

Matthew 2:11

And when they were come into the house,
they saw the young child with Mary his
mother, and fell down, and worshipped him:
and when they had opened their treasures,
they presented unto him gifts; gold, and
frankincense, and myrrh.

Matthew 10:9

Provide neither gold, nor silver, nor brass in
your purses,

Matthew 23:16

Woe unto you, [ye] blind guides, which say, Whosoever shall swear by the temple, it is nothing; but whosoever shall swear by the gold of the temple, he is a debtor!

Matthew 23:17

[Ye] fools and blind: for whether is greater, the gold, or the temple that sanctifieth the gold?

Acts 3:6

Then Peter said, Silver and gold have I none; but such as I have give I thee: In the name of Jesus Christ of Nazareth rise up and walk.

Acts 17:29

Forasmuch then as we are the offspring of God, we ought not to think that the Godhead is like unto gold, or silver, or stone, graven by art and man's device.

Acts 20:33

I have coveted no man's silver, or gold, or apparel.

Corinthians-1 3:12

Now if any man build upon this foundation gold, silver, precious stones, wood, hay, stubble;

Timothy-1 2:9

In like manner also, that women adorn themselves in modest apparel, with shamefacedness and sobriety; not with broided hair, or gold, or pearls, or costly array;

Timothy-2 2:20

But in a great house there are not only vessels of gold and of silver, but also of wood and of earth; and some to honour, and some to dishonour.

Hebrews 9:4

Which had the golden censer, and the ark of the covenant overlaid round about with gold, wherein [was] the golden pot that had manna, and Aaron's rod that budded, and the tables of the covenant;

James 2:2

For if there come unto your assembly a man with a gold ring, in goodly apparel, and there come in also a poor man in vile raiment;

James 5:3

Your gold and silver is cankered; and the rust of them shall be a witness against you, and shall eat your flesh as it were fire. Ye have heaped treasure together for the last days.

Peter-1 1:7

That the trial of your faith, being much more precious than of gold that perisheth, though it be tried with fire, might be found unto praise and honour and glory at the appearing of Jesus Christ:

Peter-1 1:18

Forasmuch as ye know that ye were not redeemed with corruptible things, [as] silver and gold, from your vain conversation [received] by tradition from your fathers;

Peter-1 3:3

Whose adorning let it not be that outward [adorning] of plaiting the hair, and of wearing of gold, or of putting on of apparel;

Revelations 3:18*

I counsel thee to buy of me gold tried in the fire, that thou mayest be rich; and white raiment, that thou mayest be clothed, and [that] the shame of thy nakedness do not appear; and anoint thine eyes with eyesalve, that thou mayest see.

Revelations 4:4

And round about the throne [were] four and twenty seats: and upon the seats I saw four and twenty elders sitting, clothed in white raiment; and they had on their heads crowns of gold.

Revelations 9:7

And the shapes of the locusts [were] like unto horses prepared unto battle; and on their heads [were] as it were crowns like gold, and their faces [were] as the faces of men.

Revelations 9:20

And the rest of the men which were not killed by these plagues yet repented not of the works of their hands, that they should not worship devils, and idols of gold, and silver, and brass, and stone, and of wood: which neither can see, nor hear, nor walk:

Revelations 17:4

And the woman was arrayed in purple and scarlet colour, and decked with gold and precious stones and pearls, having a golden cup in her hand full of abominations and filthiness of her fornication:

Revelations 18:12

The merchandise of gold, and silver, and precious stones, and of pearls, and fine linen, and purple, and silk, and scarlet, and all thyine wood, and all manner vessels of ivory, and all manner vessels of most precious wood, and of brass, and iron, and marble,

Revelations 18:16

And saying, Alas, alas, that great city, that was clothed in fine linen, and purple, and scarlet, and decked with gold, and precious stones, and pearls!

Revelations 21:18

And the building of the wall of it was [of] jasper: and the city [was] pure gold, like unto clear glass.

Revelations 21:21

And the twelve gates [were] twelve pearls: every several gate was of one pearl: and the street of the city [was] pure gold, as it were transparent glass.

Scriptures having both words counsel and gold symbolized by *